Getting Started in Calligraphy

By Nancy Baron

Sterling Publishing Co., Inc.   New York

Dedication

To David L., who got me started, and to my students, who inspired me to continue.

Library of Congress Cataloging-in-Publication Data Available

40 39 38 37 36 35 34

Published by Sterling Publishing Co., Inc.
387 Park Avenue South, New York, NY 10016
© 1979 by Sterling Publishing Co., Inc.
Distributed in Canada by Sterling Publishing
°/o Canadian Manda Group, 165 Dufferin Street,
Toronto, Ontario, Canada M6K 3H6
Distributed in Great Britain by Chrysalis Books Group PLC
The Chrysalis Building, Bramley Road, London, W10 6SP, England
Distributed in Australia by Capricorn Link (Australia) Pty. Ltd.
P.O. Box 704, Windsor, NSW 2756, Australia

Sterling ISBN 0-8069-8840-1

For information about custom editions, special sales, premium and
corporate purchases, please contact Sterling Special Sales
Department at 800-805-5489 or specialsales@sterlingpub.com.

Table of Contents

About the Author

Nancy Baron is a Larchmont, New York elementary school teacher whose calligraphy classes attract an involved and determined following. This is her first book.

About the Photographer

Michael Shelley is a resident of Larchmont, New York who enjoys working in all fields of media. This is his first professional work.

Introduction

Calligraphy comes from the Greek words, "kalos" meaning "beautiful," and "graphos" meaning "writing." The word "calligraphy" can apply to any beautiful or elegant form of writing, but calligraphers tend to use it when referring to any of the styles of writing that were in use before and during the Middle Ages in Europe. We will study two of these forms, Italics and Black Letter.

The purpose of this book is to get you started in calligraphy in the simplest, most enjoyable way possible. The lessons follow one another naturally, and are written with the easily frustrated beginner in mind. Work at your own pace. Feel free to change anything that is not comfortable for you. The suggestions and lessons in this book will guide you and help you to find your own style of writing the calligraphic alphabets. The main objective is enjoyment, not perfection. You do not have to be an artist, or even to have good penmanship, to be a successful calligrapher. In fact, your own handwriting will probably improve naturally as you progress in your lessons. Take your time, relax, and enjoy yourself.

How to Use This Book

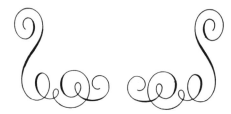

Learn any or all of the alphabets presented in this book. After you have mastered one, the others will come easily.

When learning new letters, place a piece of tracing paper or onion skin paper directly on the page of the book and trace the letters until you are familiar with them. Make sure the points you use are the same as the ones in the book. Only two points have been used in this book, the Speedball C-2, and the Speedball C-4 or Platignum Broad. The C-2 is used in sections showing how each alphabet looks, and the C-4 is used in all exercises and lessons showing how to form letters.

In the appendix you will find Master sheets with guidelines for the two different nibs, C-2 and C-4 (or Broad). Do not write directly on these sheets. Place a piece of tracing paper or onion skin paper on the master you need. The guidelines will show through. Write on the tracing paper so that you can use the master again.

Setting Up

Materials needed:

Calligraphy is not an expensive pastime, and you do not need many materials to learn it and use it. Here is a list of materials you will need:

Graph paper (¼ in.) or lined paper

Onion skin or tracing paper

Tissues

Newspaper or a desk blotter

Pen cleaner or water

Ink (fountain pen or drawing ink)

Pen and 2 nibs

> Either: a fountain pen (Platignum or Osmiroid), and 2 nibs, broad and medium

> Or: 1 pen holder and 2 Speedball nibs (C-2 and C-4 if you are right-handed, LC-2 and LC-4 if you are left-handed)

Keep your ink, extra paper, water and tissues handy but out of the way of your writing hand.

At first you will use graph or lined paper, whichever you find easier. Lay the newspaper or blotter on your writing surface to protect it in case of an accident. The writing paper will be put down next, like this:

Right-Handed   Left-handed

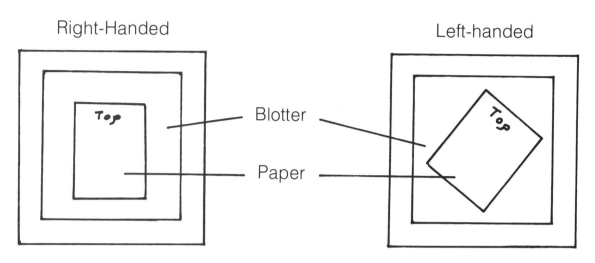

Blotter

Paper

How to Sit:

Sit up straight, but not too stiffly, squarely in front of the paper with your feet on the floor, and your arms on the writing surface.

Left-handed   Right-handed

Like this:

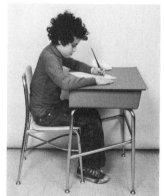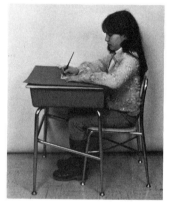

Not like this:

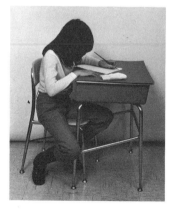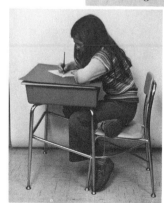

As you write, move the paper, not your body. Keep your head like this:

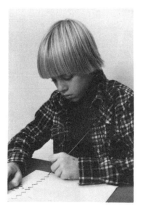

Not like this:

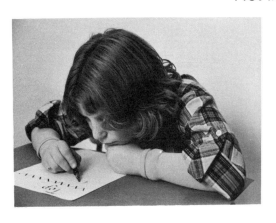 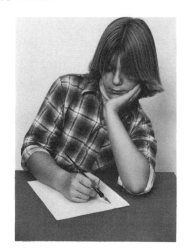

How to Hold the Pen:

When you first begin, your hand will tense up and become tired. Rest whenever you need to. Don't push yourself. Left-handed people usually have more difficulty adjusting to the pen than right-handed people. Relax and keep trying. You'll get it.

Try not to hold the pen too tightly.

Hold it like this:

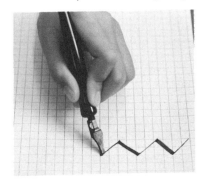

Not like this:

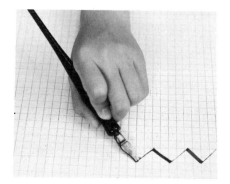

Pen and hand too close to the paper

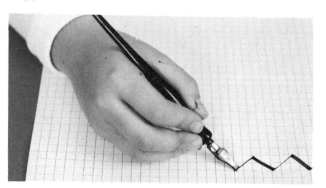

Middle finger on top of the pen

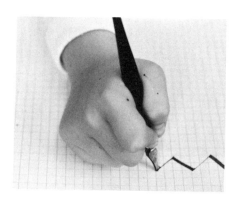

Thumb wrapped around

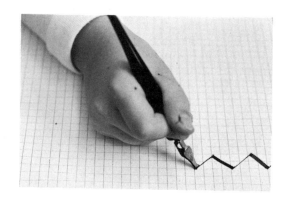

Pen held in a fist

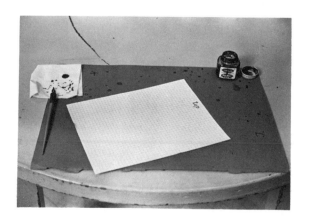

Using a pen holder, nib and ink:

1. Put the nib into the pen so that it fits securely.
2. Dip the point into the ink so that the ink comes about halfway up the point.
3. Dab the filled point onto a tissue, getting rid of some of the ink, so that you don't get too much ink on the paper. Soon you will be able to tell just how much ink you can dab off and still have enough left on the pen to write several letters.
4. Be careful not to put too much pressure on the point. Press down just hard enough to get a good strong line of ink on the paper. If you can't see the writing inscribed on the point of the pen, you're holding the pen upside down.
5. After using the nib, clean it by dipping it into the pen cleaner and/or water and wiping it dry gently with a tissue.

Using a fountain pen and ink:

1. Fill the pen with ink made for a fountain pen, such as Sheaffer, Pelican or Parker. Do not use any brand of India ink. There are special inks made for calligraphy. They are very strong and flow slowly for a sharp line, but tend to clog up in the pen when the pen is not flushed out often with water.
2. When you need to change nibs or ink, clean out the pen first with pen cleaner and/or water.
3. Keep the cap on the pen and carry it with the cap up so the pen doesn't leak.
4. Be careful not to injure the point. Don't put too much pressure on it as you write.
5. Wipe off the point gently after each use before you put on the cap. Lint from the paper may become stuck in the nib, causing the ink to spread out too much on the paper.

Holding the pen at the correct angle:

All of the alphabets in this book require that you hold the pen at a 45° angle, like this:

 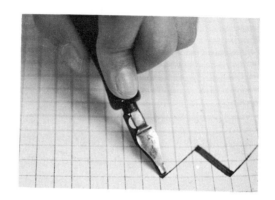

This angle is very important. If you don't keep your pen point at a consistent, correct angle as you write, your letters will look incorrect, even if you form them correctly. Right-handed people should keep their right elbow away from their body. Left-handed writers should keep their elbow close to their body, and should avoid hooking their hand. The top of the pen should point towards the right shoulder no matter what hand you use.

Avoid these mistakes:

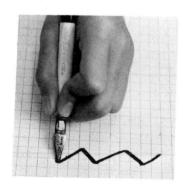

Not a 45° angle

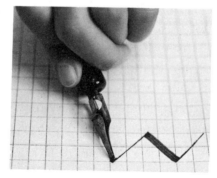

Writing with edge of point

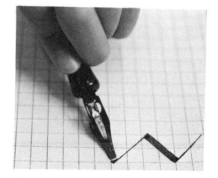

Point is upside down

Loosening-Up Exercises

These exercises will help you hold the pen at the correct angle, and will give you a chance to practice some of the strokes used in Italics and Black Letter.

1) Holding your pen at the correct angle, make this design:

(Use the broad nib at first.)

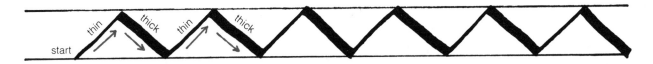

If you are holding your pen correctly, your up strokes will be thin, and your down strokes will be thick. Repeat this "thin-thick" exercise until you are comfortable with the pen and ink, and are sure of the angle. You can use this as a warm-up exercise each time you sit down to write.

2) Keeping your pen at a 45° angle, make long and short strokes:

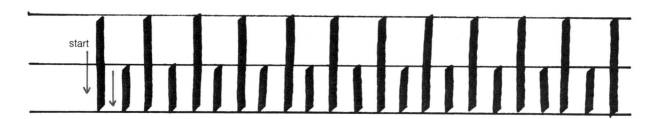

Notice the points at the top and bottom of each stroke: 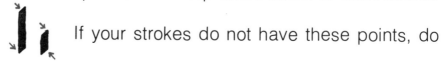 If your strokes do not have these points, do the "thin-thick" exercise until you once more have a 45° angle. Also, be sure to keep the whole point of the nib on the paper at all times. Do not write with the edge of the point.

3) Concentrating on the angle of the pen, make triangles like these:

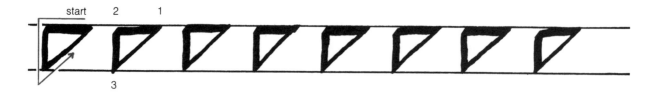

Begin at 1, then push the pen to 2, come straight down to 3, and up at an angle to 1 again. Notice the thick and thin lines. If they are in the wrong places, go back to exercises 1 and 2 and work on the angle of the pen again. This exercise will help with the formation of many letters.

4) Relax your hand and do a page of these:

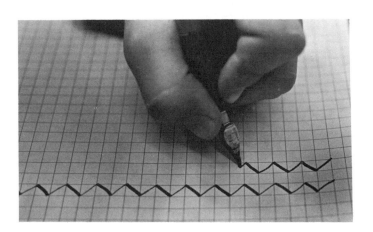

Move your arm, not your fingers.

Now you are ready to learn your first calligraphic alphabet.

Italics

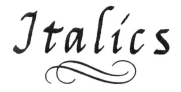

Italic lettering is the most popular form of calligraphy. It flourished in western Europe at the time of the Renaissance. The famous Italian artist Michelangelo was proud of his fine Italic handwriting.

We will begin with the Chancery Cursive alphabet, since it is considered by many calligraphers to be the most beautiful Italic style. There is a slight slant (10°) to the letters, which are oval, rather than round, in form. The long extensions on the tops and bottoms of the letters (called ascenders and descenders) are bent over a great deal.

Begin by lining your paper. The lines should be 5 pen widths apart, like this:

5 pen widths {
5 pen widths {
5 pen widths {

(You can easily line your paper by tracing the Master for Italics on page 90.) When we talk about pen widths, we mean the width of the pen nib, or point.

Chancery Cursive

Here is what the lower case Chancery Cursive alphabet looks like:

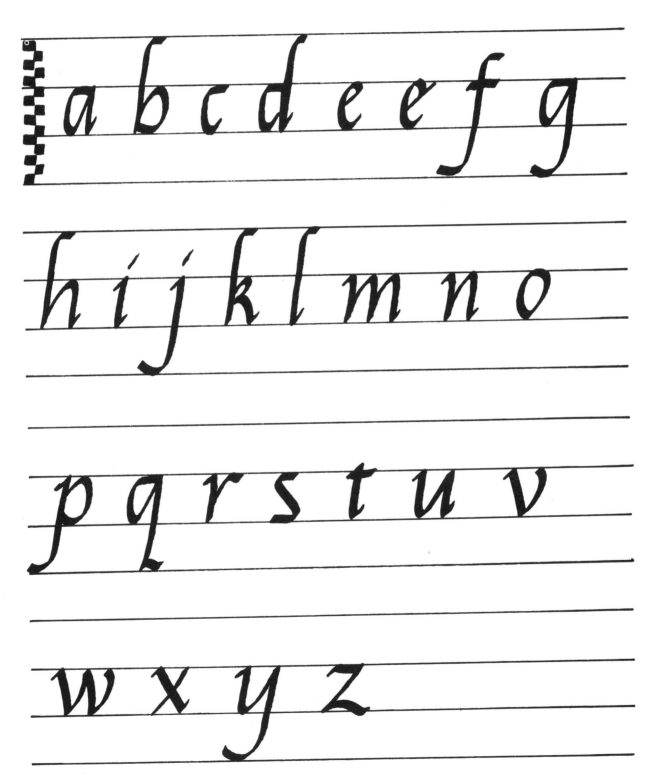

a b c d e e f g

h i j k l m n o

p q r s t u v

w x y z

All the letters are the same width except *i, j, l,*

m & *w* (The first 3 are narrower and the last 2 are wider than the other letters.)

We will learn Chancery Cursive in six lessons. This is to keep you from doing too much at once. At first you will become tired quickly and your fingers will ache. Rest when you are tired, and flex your fingers every now and then. Remember:

1) Keep your paper straight if you are right-handed, slanted towards the right if you are left-handed. (See page 8.)

2) Keep your pen at a 45° angle.

3) Sit properly.

4) Don't grip the pen too tightly.

5) Relax.

Place a piece of tracing paper or onion skin paper on the page and trace the letters until you are comfortable with them. Then use tracing paper over the Master sheet guidelines (on pages 88 to 92) to practice letters and words on your own.

Lesson 1: l,i,t,r,n,m,h,b,k,j,p.

Practice each letter until you are comfortable with it:

l l l *bend* l *lift quickly* l   i i i *lift quickly* i   t t t *two strokes* t *lift quickly*

Some common mistakes:

lit   lit   lit   lit

correct   too round   too pointed   flip the ends by lifting the pen quickly

Practice these combinations:

ill   till   lilt   tilt

r r r *lift quickly* r   n n n *thin line* n *lift quickly*   m m m *thin line* m *almost pointed*

Some common mistakes:

rnm   rnm   rnm   rnm

correct   too narrow   too wide   too pointed

Practice these, then make up your own combinations:

rim   mitt   in   mill   tin

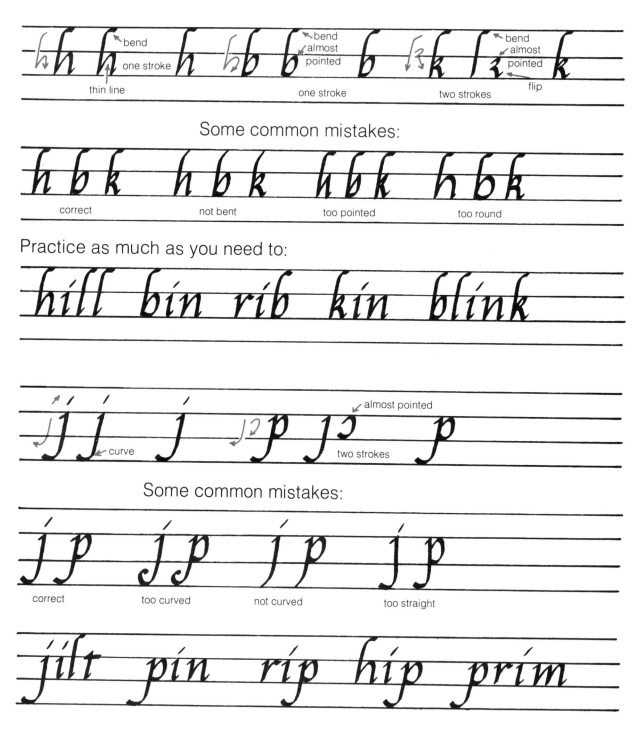

Some common mistakes:

correct   not bent   too pointed   too round

Practice as much as you need to:

hill bin rib kin blink

Some common mistakes:

correct   too curved   not curved   too straight

jilt pin rip hip prim

When you are comfortable with these, go on to Lesson 2.

Lesson 2: u, y, v, w, s.

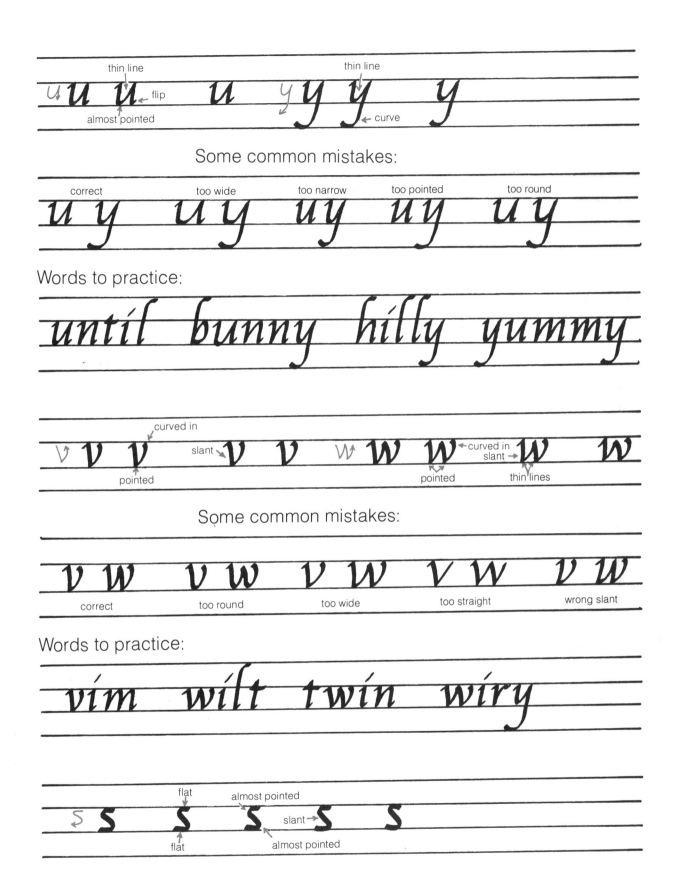

thin line   thin line

u u u — flip   u   y y y ← curve   y

almost pointed

Some common mistakes:

| correct | too wide | too narrow | too pointed | too round |

u y   u y   u y   u y   u y

Words to practice:

until bunny hilly yummy

curved in

v v v   slant ↘   v   v   w   w ← curved in slant → w   w

pointed   pointed   thin lines

Some common mistakes:

v w   v w   v w   v w   v w

correct   too round   too wide   too straight   wrong slant

Words to practice:

vim wilt twin wiry

flat   almost pointed

s s s slant → s s

flat   almost pointed

Some common mistakes:

S	S	S	S	S
correct	too round	too pointed	ends out too far	ends in too far

Practice carefully, then go on to Lesson 3:

stilts mississippi kiss swim

Lesson 3: c, o, d, e or e, a, g, q.

push pen left   flat   start here

C C C C O O slight curve O O keep oval shape

almost pointed   almost pointed

Some common mistakes:

co	co	co	co	co	co
correct	too pointed	too round	too wide	too square	too slanted

Practice:

cop city coop scissors our

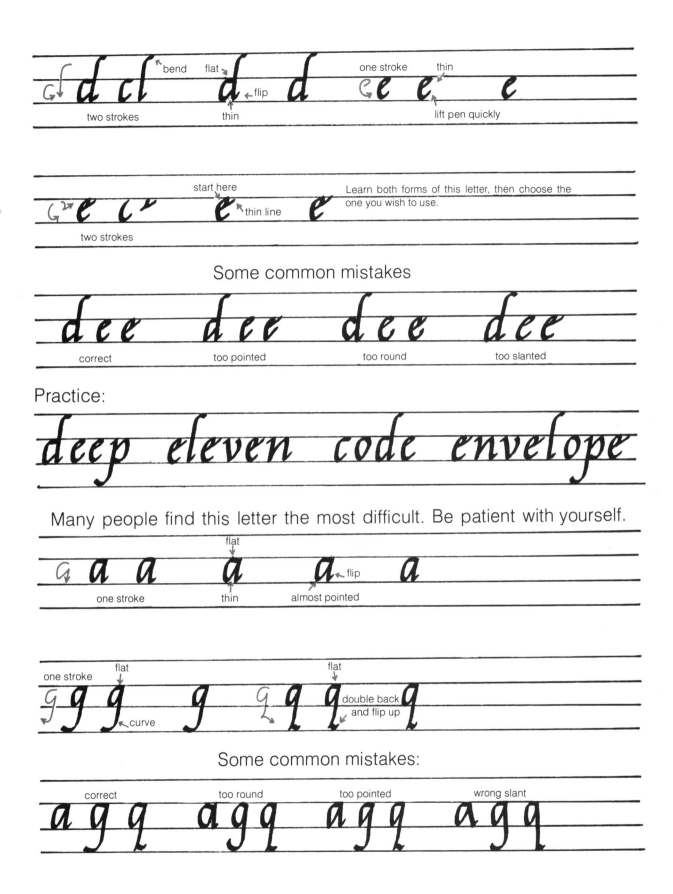

bend   flat   one stroke   thin

two strokes   thin   lift pen quickly

start here   Learn both forms of this letter, then choose the one you wish to use.

thin line

two strokes

Some common mistakes

correct   too pointed   too round   too slanted

Practice:

deep eleven code envelope

Many people find this letter the most difficult. Be patient with yourself.

flat

one stroke   thin   almost pointed   flip

one stroke   flat   flat

curve   double back and flip up

Some common mistakes:

correct   too round   too pointed   wrong slant

Make up words and practice them until you are ready for Lesson 4.

agree quill aqua night egg

Lesson 4: x, z, f

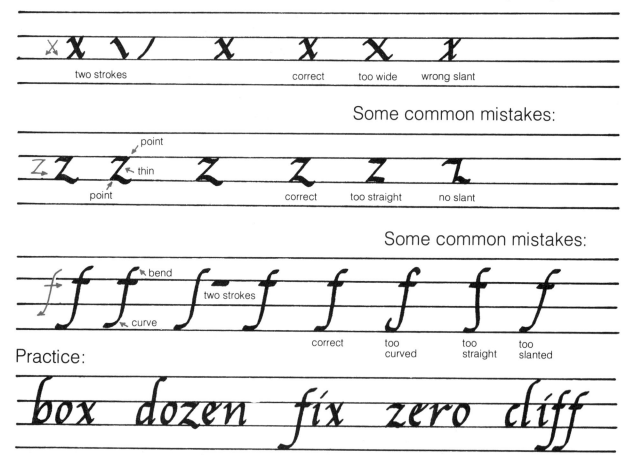

Some common mistakes:

X X / X X X X
two strokes   correct too wide wrong slant

Some common mistakes:

point
Z Z Z thin Z Z Z Z
point   correct too straight no slant

Some common mistakes:

bend
f f f two strokes f f f f f
curve   correct too too too
         curved straight slanted

Practice:

box dozen fix zero cliff

Go back and practice any letters that are still giving you a hard time. Then try this sentence before going on to Lesson 5:

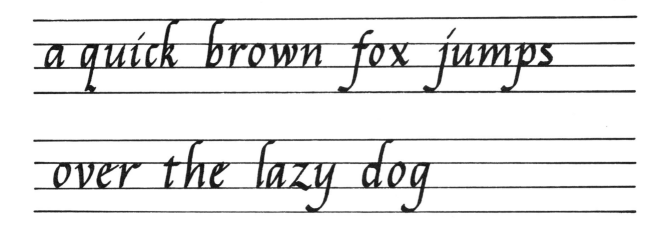

Lesson 5: Joining Letters

When writing something that will be on display, it is best not to join the letters. This is when beauty is more important than speed. When a little more speed is called for, in everyday handwriting chores such as the making of lists or letter-writing, knowing how to join letters is desirable. As you learn how to make your joinings, keep the following simple rules in mind:

1) Keep your joining lines light and thin. Lift your pen slightly when joining.

2) Don't try to join every letter with one stroke. People join letters to write faster and more efficiently, but don't sacrifice beauty for speed if you can help it.

3) Try different ways to join letters until you have found the ones that suit you best, then use them consistently.

The following patterns and exercises will help you find the most comfortable ways to join your letters.

Group 1—Letters that end on the up stroke:

a c d h i k l m n u

Continue the up stroke until it becomes the down stroke of the letters in Group 2.

Group 2—Letters that begin on the up stroke:

i j m n p r t u v w x y

Group 3—Letters which can be joined with the letters before them just by having them touch on the way down:

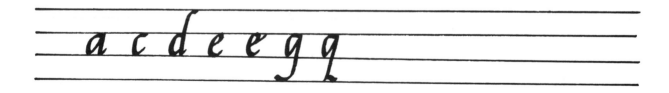
a c d e e g g

Examples of joining letters from Group 1 with those from Group 2:

ai it at mp ar hu aw ly

nu him cup lump dummy

Examples of joining letters from Group 1 with those from Group 3:

ca de ng ia lag ace mad

b, l, h & k are not joined to the letters before them.

l, h & k are in Group 1, therefore they can be joined to letters that come after them.

b looks best not joined at either end.

all chalk band nimbly ink

g, y, j & *q* are not joined to the letters following them, unless you choose to make the tail into a loop.

gap yam quit jar

e is joined like *c* at both ends. *e* is joined like the *c* to the letters before it, but has its own special join with the letters that come after it. Choose which version you want to use, then use it consistently.

bend bend leg leg net net

Cross the *t* & *f* before you join them with the next letter. Sometimes it's *f* best not to try to join them, especially to each other.

fit tin fun tun after

Join the *o* to another letter when it is natural to do so.

look on for out or *out color*

Do not try to join the *s* with another letter in one continuous line with this alphabet. It can appear to be joined with a letter when it comes after a letter from Group 1.

lift   lift   lift   lift

as us is son snow pass

The *r* joins more easily with letters that come before it than with those that come after it. Go with what you think looks best.

rob run fire trap ours

The *v, w, x* & *z* look best when joined only at the beginning stroke.

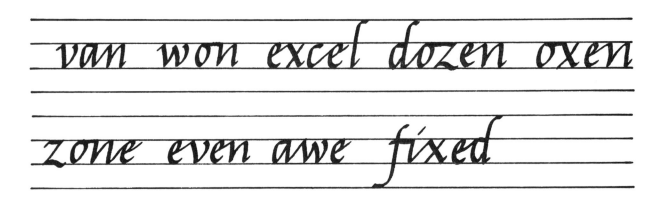

van won excel dozen oxen

zone even awe fixed

Here is that sentence that uses every letter in the alphabet. Make up and practice some sentences of your own. Keep your join lines thin and light.

a quick brown fox jumps

over the lazy dog

Lesson 6: Capitals

You have probably looked ahead to this section so that you could write your names and the names of friends. I've saved the capitals for last because they are easy once you've learned the lower case letters, and because they just aren't considered as important. You can make up your own. I've used as examples two types—one plain and one fancy. Change them any way you wish.

First, you should know that Italic capitals are about ¾ as high as a lower case *l*, or 7 pen widths high:

Don't bother measuring: Just keep them a little shorter than the top line of your lined paper.

Inger Gary Janeen Timothy Nancy

Lara Bowen

A B C D E F G

H I J K L M N

O P Q R S T U

V W X Y Z

Flourished Capitals: Be loose and free.

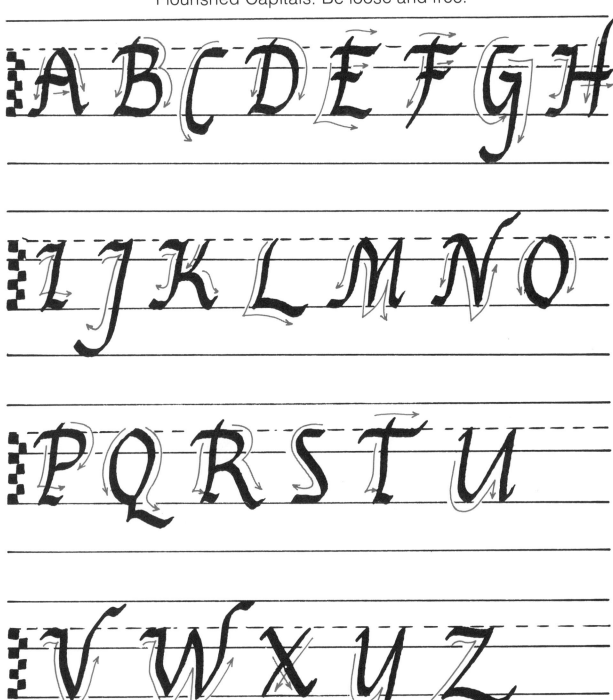

Lisa Paul Nancy Ron

Kate John Betsy Tom

Gail Charles Vera Ian

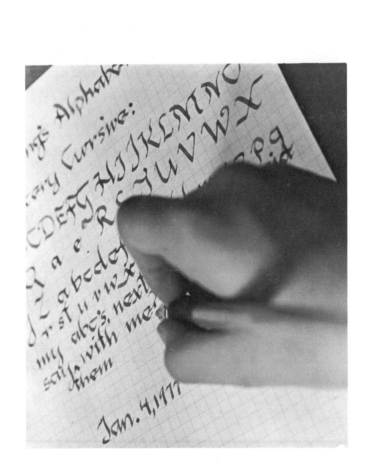

Formal Italic

Here is what the lower case Formal Italic alphabet looks like.

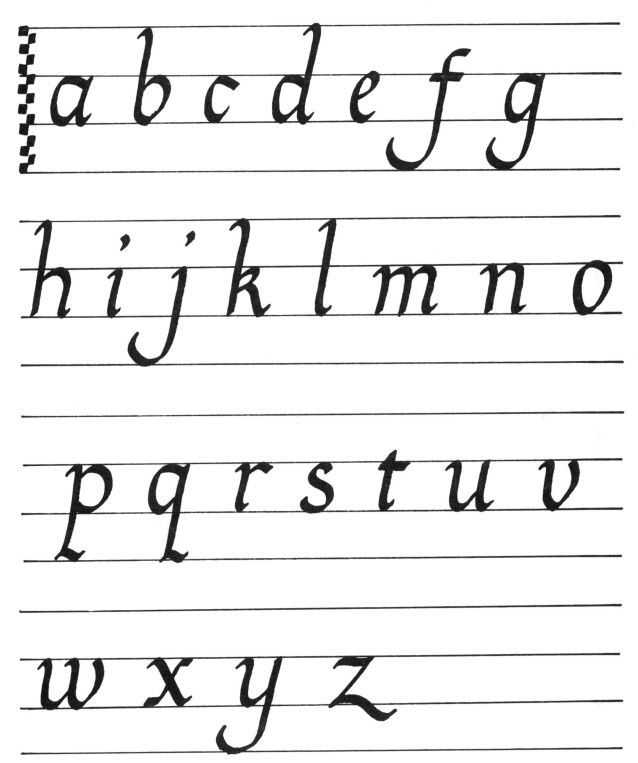

The Formal, or Humanistic Italic letters have the same slant and proportions as Chancery Cursive. Many calligraphers prefer this style for its simple elegance.

As you can see, the letters are a little more rounded than in Chancery Cursive, though they are still based on the oval. The beginnings of the letters with long ascenders are bent to the left instead of the right, as in Chancery, and they aren't bent as much. The descenders make much more of a hook than they did in Chancery. You have to lift your pen more often as you form Formal Italic letters than you did for Chancery Cursive.

This time there will be five lessons, many of them similar to those in the Chancery Cursive section. Follow the same basic rules. The differences between the two alphabets will be clear as you proceed.

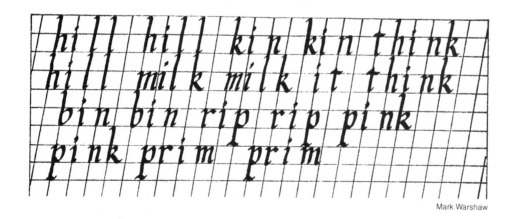

Mark Warshaw

Lesson 1: l, i, t, r, n, m, h, k, b, p.

Make your strokes loose and smooth:

l l l *slightly rounded*   l   i i i i *slightly rounded*   i   t t t *curve*   t

two strokes

ill till lilt tilt it

r r r *two strokes*   r   n n n *thin line* *two strokes*   n   m m m *thin line* *three strokes*   m

rim mitt in mill tin

h h h *two strokes*   h   k k k *three strokes*   k

hill kin think milk hit

37

b l' b thin *p l₁² p* *b*

two strokes

three strokes

If you would like
to try one stroke,
go ahead.

bin rip pink bill prim

When you are sure of these letters, go on to Lesson 2.

Lesson 2: u, y, v, w, j, f, s.

two strokes two strokes

u u u y y y

thin big curve

until bunny pull hilly

v v v w w w

two strokes three strokes

vim twin will wiry

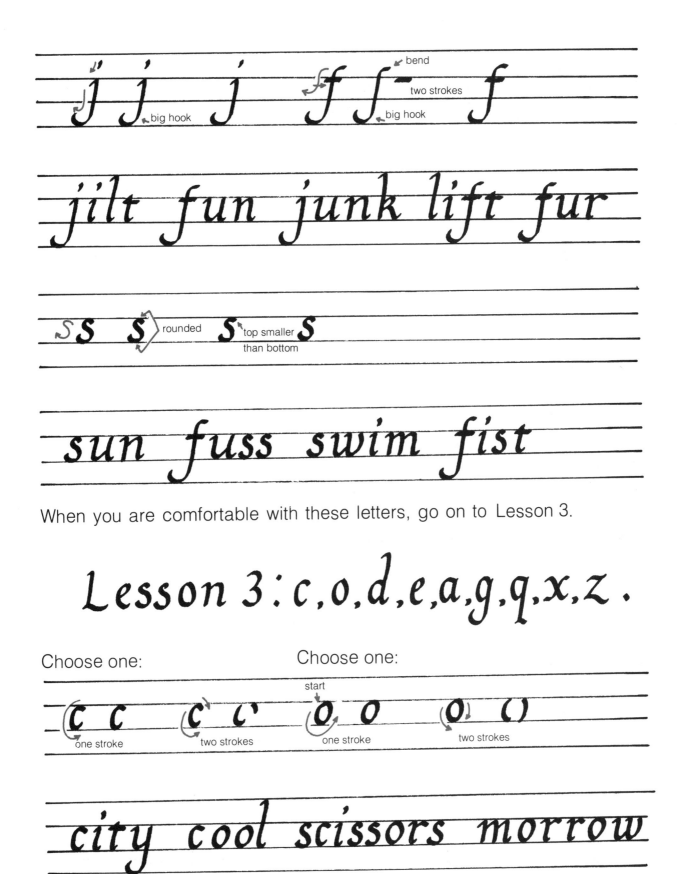

j j j ← bend f f f
↗ big hook   two strokes ← big hook

jilt fun junk lift fur

s s s rounded s top smaller s
than bottom

sun fuss swim fist

When you are comfortable with these letters, go on to Lesson 3.

Lesson 3: c, o, d, e, a, g, q, x, z.

Choose one: Choose one:

start
(c c   (c c   (o o   (o ()
one stroke   two strokes   one stroke   two strokes

city cool scissors morrow

Choose one and keep it.

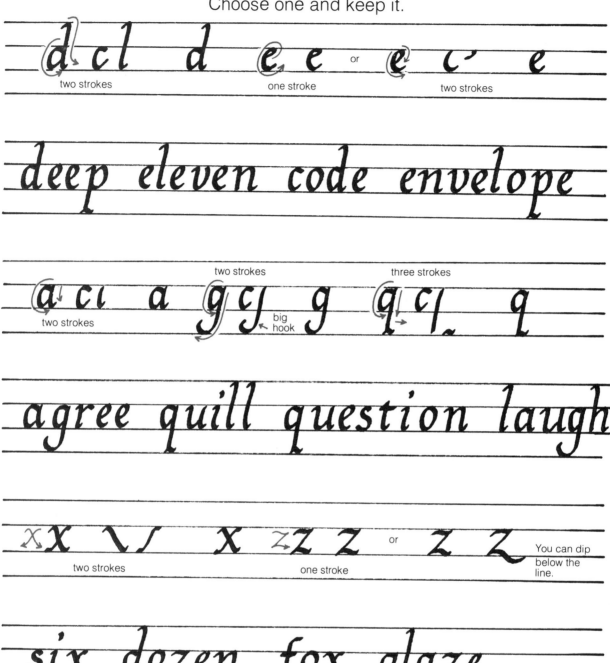

two strokes   one stroke   or   two strokes

deep eleven code envelope

two strokes   three strokes

two strokes   big hook

agree quill question laugh

two strokes   one stroke   or   You can dip below the line.

six dozen fox glaze

Make sure you know these letters well before you try to join them.

Lesson 4: Joining Letters

The rules for joining these letters are the same as those for Chancery Cursive letters (see page 25). The patterns for the types of letters are also the same, therefore they should be joined in the same way. I will deal here with some of the exceptions, and will give you examples illustrating joinings made in Formal Italics.

Examples of joining letters from Group 1 with those from Group 2:

ai it at mp ar hu aw

ty nu him cup lump

dummy aim

Examples of joining letters from Group 1 with those from Group 3:

ca de ng ia lag ace eel

b, l, h & k:

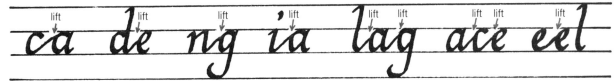

all chalk band nimbly

q · g · y & *j* :

gap yam quit jar

You can loop the tails of the last 3 letters if you like.

gap yam jar

Keep the joining loops as thin and light as possible.

t & *f* :

fit tin fan tan after

o : (made with one stroke)

look on for out color

o: (made with two strokes)

look on for out color

s:

^{lift} ^{lift} ^{lift} ^{lift} ^{lift}
as us is ask son snow pass

r:

rob run run fire traps

v, w, x & z:

van won oxen dozen awe

zone even fixed

Compare:

Individual letters:

a quick brown fox jumps

over the lazy dog

Joined letters:

a quick brown fox jumps

over the lazy dog

Lesson 5: Capitals

Following are two more sets of Italic capitals:
one simple, the second flourished.

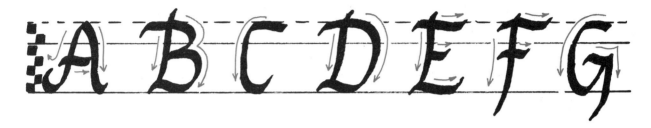

ABCDEFG

HIJKLM

NOPQRST

UVWXYZ

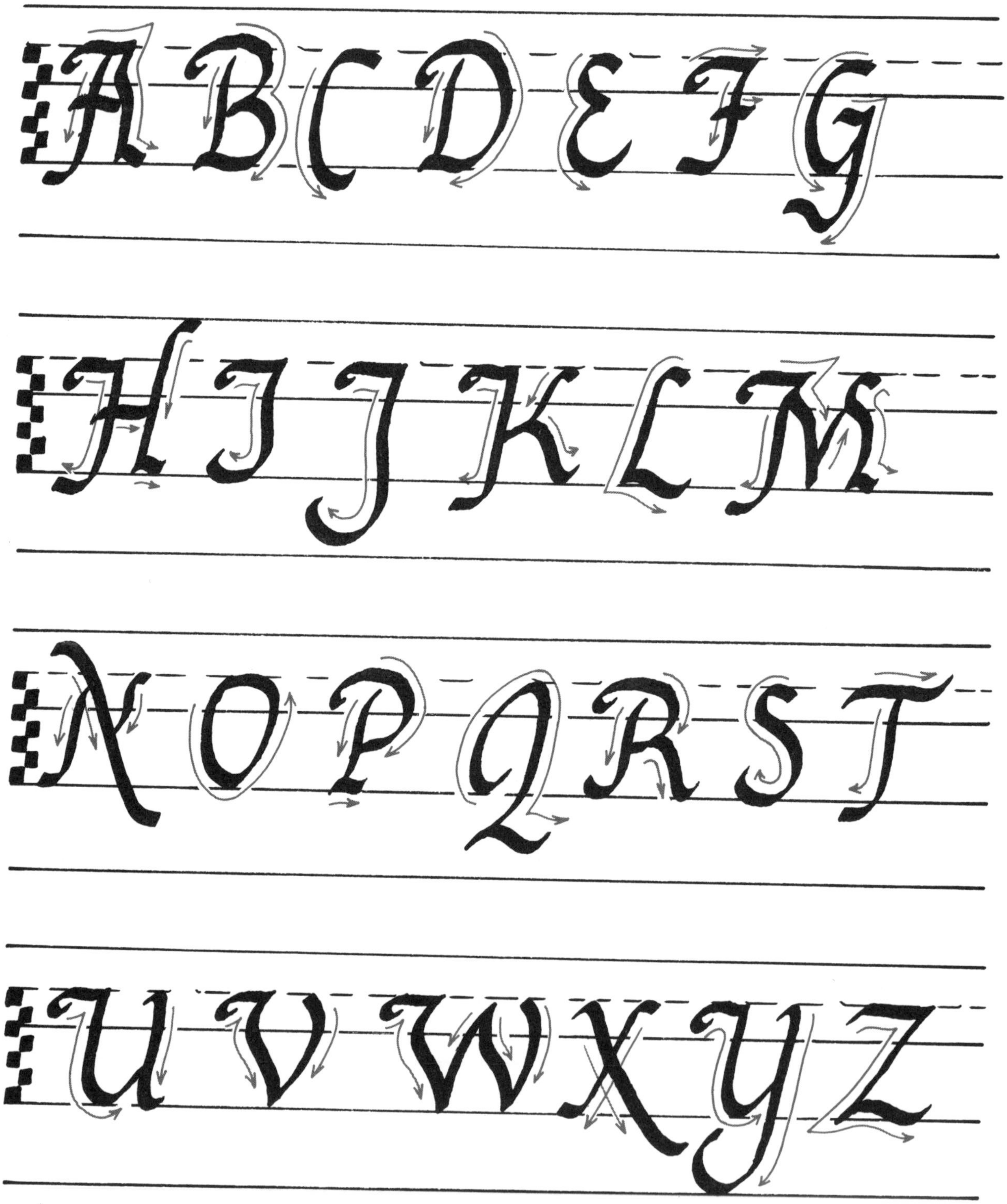

ABCDEFG

HIJKLM

NOPQRST

UVWXYZ

Use either of the two alphabets shown in the Chancery Cursive section (see pages 32 and 33), or try one of these. Feel free to change them in any way. The size and proportions are the same as the two you've already tried.

Mix and match the capitals, extend their lines, etc., but don't make them so outrageous that you overpower the letters that follow them.

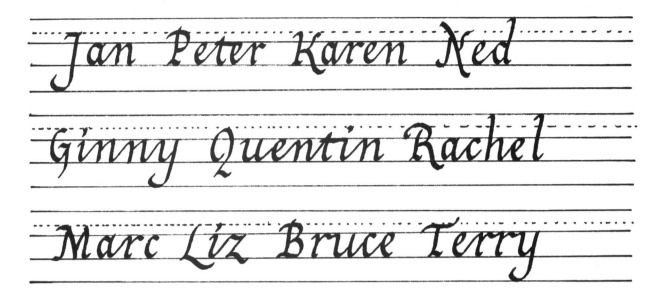

Jan Peter Karen Ned

Ginny Quentin Rachel

Marc Liz Bruce Terry

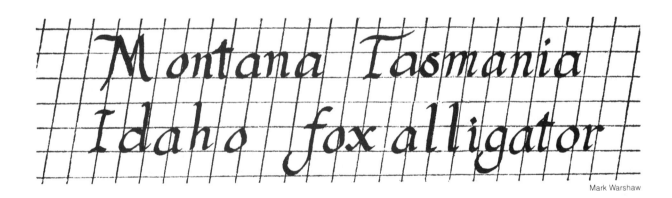

Montana Tasmania Idaho fox alligator

Mark Warshaw

Straight, or Practical Italics

Here is what the lower case Straight Italics alphabet looks like:

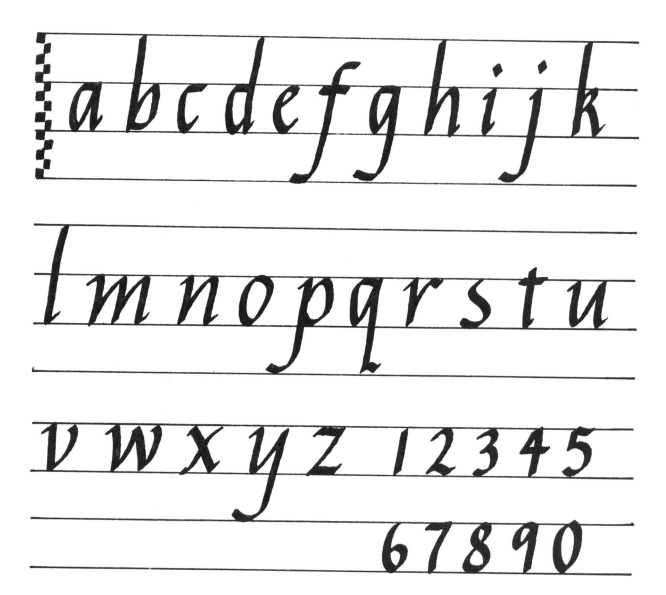

In shape this alphabet is very much like Chancery Cursive. The biggest difference is that these letters do not have bent ascenders. Some people who really want to be efficient leave out the bends in the descenders as well. Follow the rules for Chancery Cursive when forming these letters.

If you want to use Italics all the time as your everyday handwriting, this is the style to learn. It is the most practical and efficient, with no wasted strokes. It has the same slant, proportions, and oval shape as Chancery Cursive and Formal.

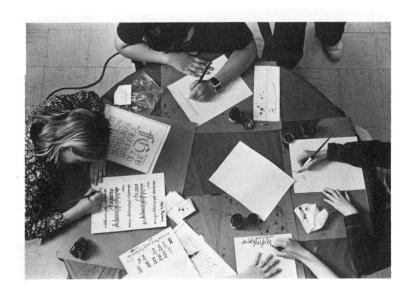

Lesson 1: l,i,t,r,n,m,h,b,k,j,p,f.

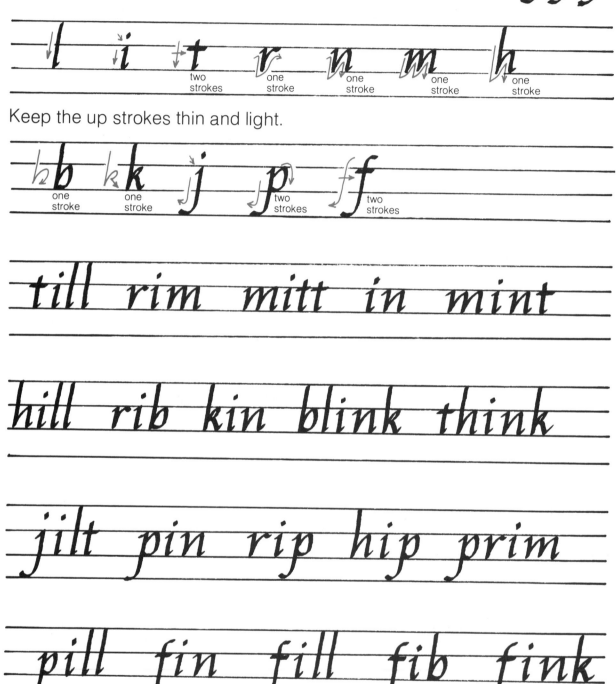

l   i   t   r   n   m   h
two strokes   one stroke   one stroke   one stroke   one stroke

Keep the up strokes thin and light.

b   k   j   p   f
one stroke   one stroke   two strokes   two strokes

till rim mitt in mint

hill rib kin blink think

jilt pin rip hip prim

pill fin fill fib fink

You can simplify the descenders. Do what is comfortable for you.

j p jilt pin rip jib

f f fill fin fill fin

Lesson 2: u, y, v, w, s.

All one stroke:

u y v w s s   Smaller on the top than on the bottom.

until bunny hilly fun

vim wilt twin stilts sun

mississippi kiss swim

Lesson 3: c, o, d, e, a, g, q.

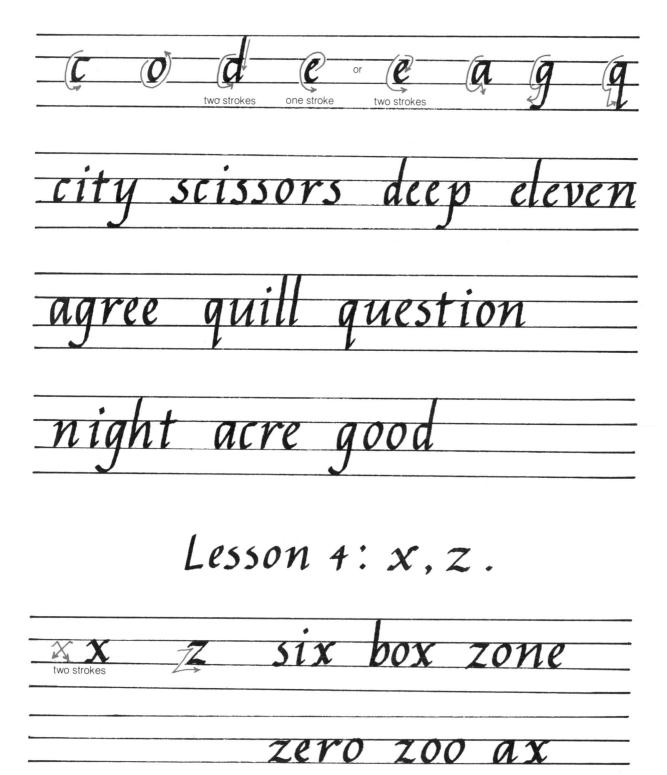

c o d e *or* e a g q

two strokes · one stroke · two strokes

city scissors deep eleven

agree quill question

night acre good

Lesson 4: x, z.

x x z z six box zone

two strokes

zero zoo ax

Lesson 5: Joining Letters

Since this alphabet is designed for speed as well as beauty, more letters may be joined. Use your own judgment, but keep in mind the rules mentioned in the joining lesson in Chancery Cursive (see page 25).

Examples of joining letters from Group 1 with letters from Group 2:

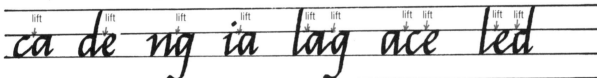

Examples of joining letters from Group 1 with letters from Group 3:

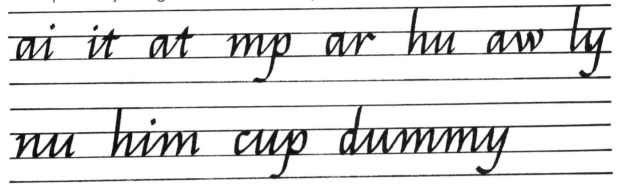

or, if you are in a hurry and have a delicate touch:

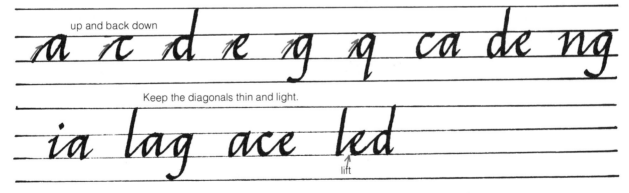

Most of these letters are in the same groups, and are joined in the same way as those in Chancery Cursive, so refer back to that section whenever necessary. The differences and similarities will become obvious immediately.

b, l, h & k :

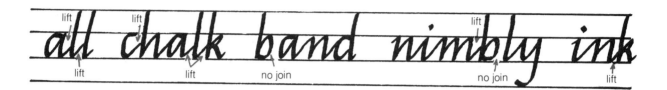

all chalk band nimbly ink

g, y, j & q :

gap *or* gap yam *or* yam

quit jar

e made with one stroke is joined like the *c* at both ends.

e made with two strokes is joined to the letters after it so that it is like the *e* of Chancery Cursive. Again, choose the one you prefer, and keep it.

bend *or* bend leg *or* leg net *or* net

t & *f*:

cross once   cross once

tin fun after little baffle

o:

o o o look on for out color

s: You have a few possibilities:

s or *s* or *s* as or as us or us is or is

son or son pass or pass or pass

r: Whether or not you join is up to you.

rob run fire trap pours

v, w, x & z :

v v w w van won even

weave excel dozen ox zoo

A reminder: I am showing examples of both kinds of e's.
You may use either one, but try to be consistent about it.
When it falls at the end of a letter, you also have a choice:

For example *one* or *one* if you use two
strokes, but only *one* if you use one stroke.

a quick brown fox jumps

over the lazy dog

If you are tired of that sentence, here is another one that uses all the letters of the alphabet. Put in the capitals if you wish.

lucy got experience

attaching buttons and

zippers in quebec, and she

would love to make a

jacket for you

composed by Nicole Cusick

Lesson 6: Capitals

In your everyday handwriting, use the simple capitals in the Chancery Cursive section (see page 32). For work that is more special use any of the flourished capitals in that section (see page 33) or in the Formal Italic section (see page 46), or make up your own. Not too fancy, though.

Fred Susan Gary Barbara

Mel Carol Dennis Vicki

Adam Eve Hal Olive

Numerals:

Make your numerals as simple or flourished as you wish. Here are some suggestions. Write them between the lines, or extend them above or below the base lines. Use your own judgment.

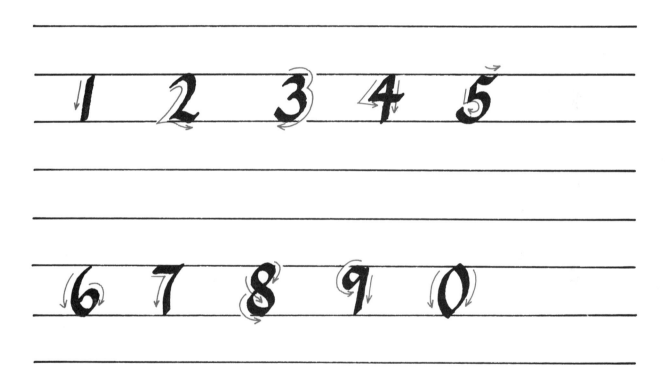

You have now finished the Italics section of this book. Practice, experiment, and use it whenever you can. Try each alphabet, then choose one to make your own. Feel free to change the basic letters to suit your own style. On the following pages you will find some special exercises to help you practice your strokes, and some examples of how a few young calligraphers fared with their introduction to Italics.

Special Exercises ~ Borders

Borders add to the beauty of invitations, letters, posters, and works of display. Draw equal margins around your paper and use these lines for the guidelines of your borders.

Guidelines for Border

Here are some simple designs for borders that will help you practice your strokes. Practice these, then make up some of your own.

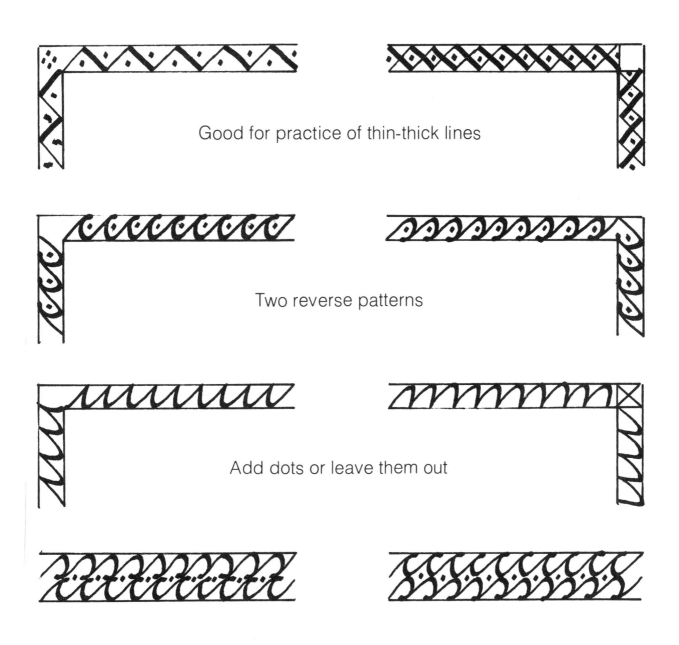

Good for practice of thin-thick lines

Two reverse patterns

Add dots or leave them out

Double them up

Samples of Italics

out out out out color color color color
top top top top as as as as us us us us
pours van van van van van won won won
won excel excel excel excel dozen dozen
dozen oxen zone zone zone zone even

Eve Rittenberg

box dozen zone
glaze zerofor fix

life loaf stiff
cliff even help
kkaty

Lara Bowen

She wondered what
was wrong
His back was to her
She tryed to imagine
what was wrong
He walked away
He held a secret
which no one
knew
They tryed to find
out
They didn't
No one cares anymore

Liz Shilling

 Black Letter

Black Letter, also known as Gothic or Old English, was used for religious writings. Today we can see it on diplomas, letterheads, and signs. The letters are straight and tall, and are used for decoration only, since they take longer to form and are more difficult to read than Italics.

We will look at two Black Letter alphabets. The first one is very angular and heavy-looking. The second one is a little more rounded and delicate in appearance.

Keep the pen at the same 45° angle that you used for Italics, but instead of writing with a slight slant to the letters, keep them as vertical as possible. The main part of each letter is 5 pen widths high, as in Italics, but the ascenders are 4 pen widths high, and the descenders are 3 pen widths below the line:

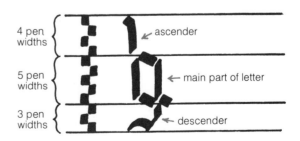

Here are some important rules to keep in mind when writing in Black Letter. These rules apply to both types of Black Letter alphabets learned.

1) Keep the down strokes straight and parallel with each other:

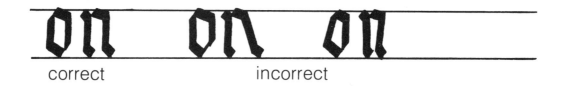

correct   incorrect

2) Keep the pen at a 45° angle at all times:

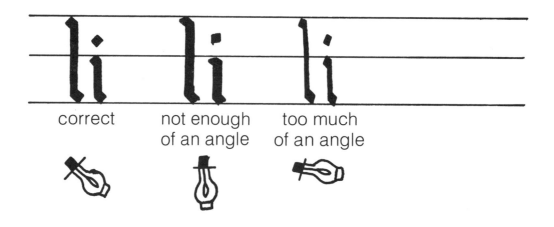

correct   not enough   too much
          of an angle   of an angle

3) Pay careful attention to the spaces inside and between the letters:

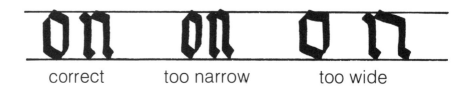

correct   too narrow   too wide

4) Connect the different strokes of the letters by having
   them barely touch each other at the corners:

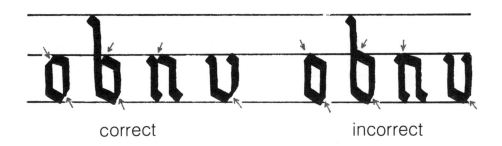

correct   incorrect

The warm-up exercises in the "Loosening-Up" section of this book (see page 13) will help you in Black Letter as well as Italics. Here are four additional exercises that will prepare you for the strokes used in Black Letter.

Do these exercises until you are comfortable with them. Then go on to the first Black Letter alphabet.

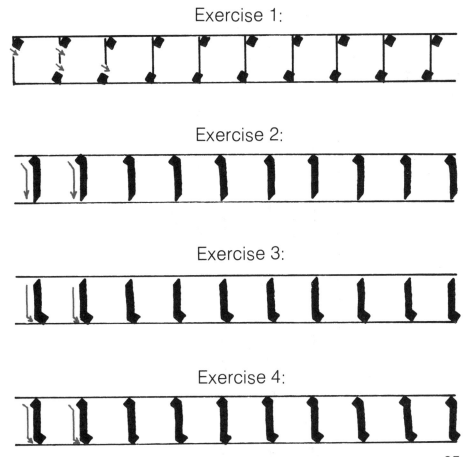

Exercise 1:

Exercise 2:

Exercise 3:

Exercise 4:

Straight Black Letter

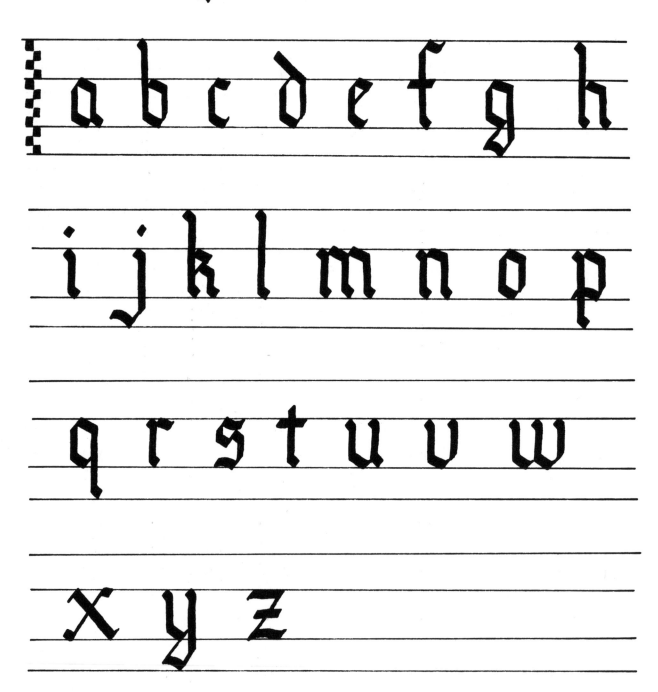

These are the lower case letters in the Straight Black Letter alphabet. You will learn the alphabet in five lessons.

Lesson 1: l, i, t, r, n, m, h.

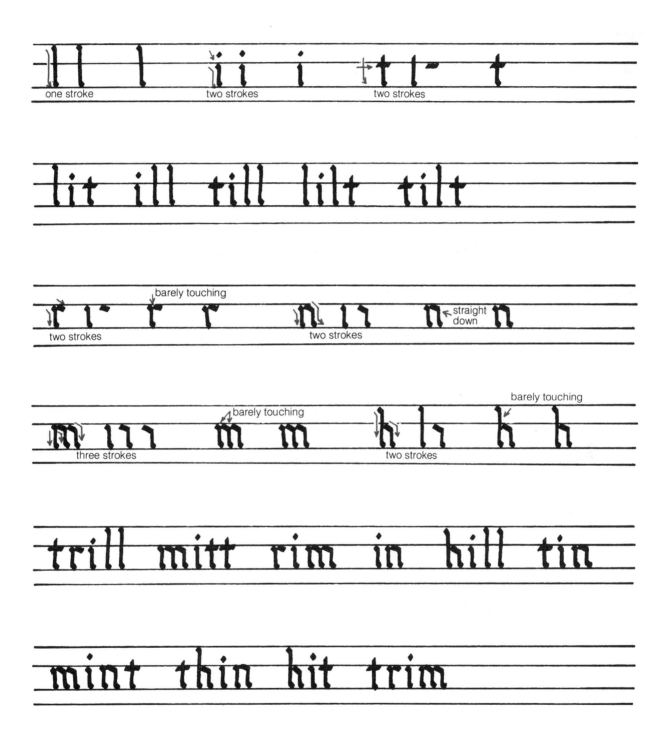

Lesson 2: u, v, w.

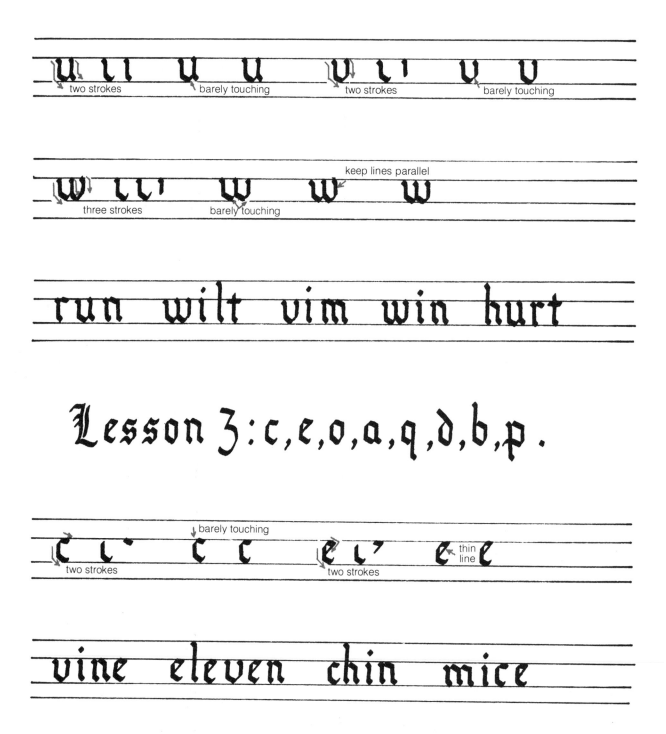

two strokes   barely touching   two strokes   barely touching

three strokes   barely touching   keep lines parallel

run wilt vim win hurt

Lesson 3: c, e, o, a, q, d, b, p.

barely touching

two strokes   two strokes   thin line

vine eleven chin mice

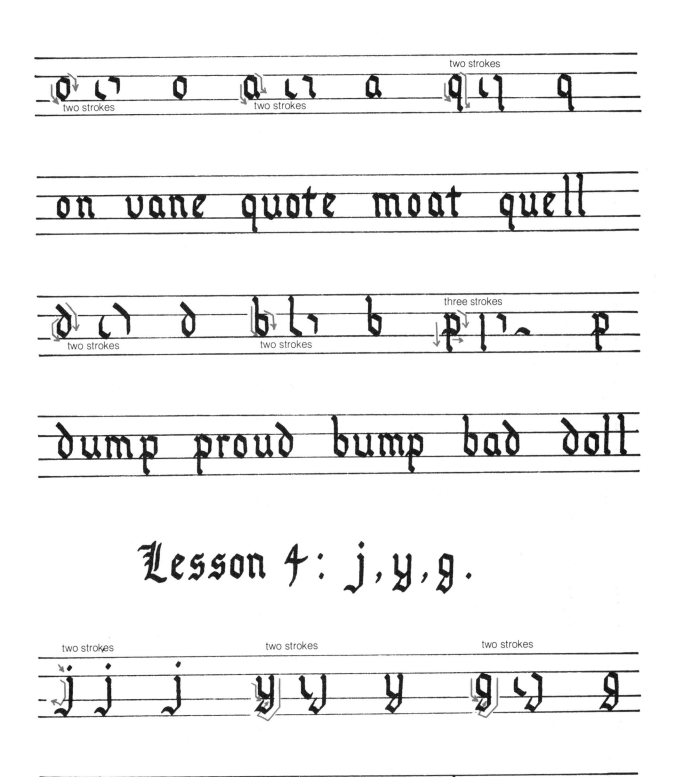

on vane quote moat quell

dump proud bump bad doll

Lesson 4: j, y, g.

jelly judge guppy bug yam

Lesson 5: x, z, f, k, s.

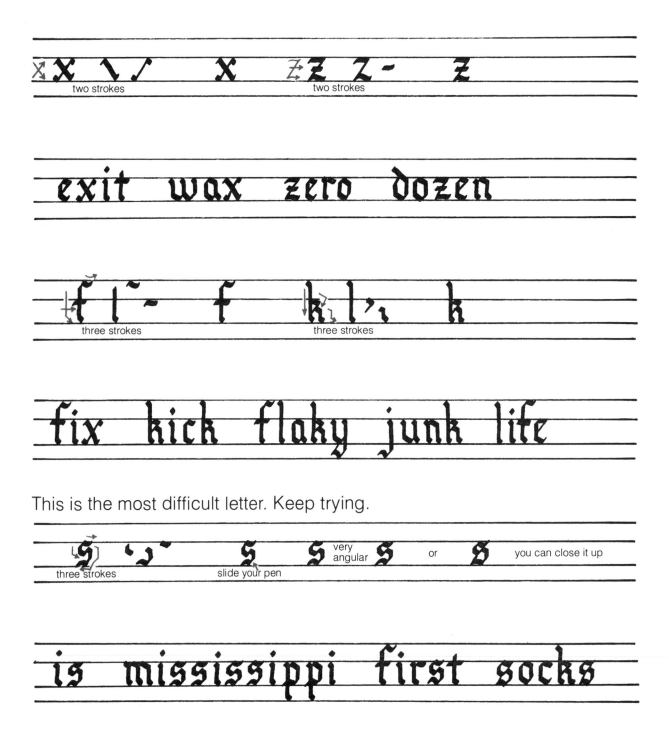

two strokes   two strokes

exit wax zero dozen

three strokes   three strokes

fix kick flaky junk life

This is the most difficult letter. Keep trying.

three strokes   slide your pen   very angular   or   you can close it up

is mississippi first socks

a quick brown fox jumps

over the lazy dog

lucy got experience attaching

buttons and zippers in quebec,

and she would love to make

a jacket for you

You will find the capitals at the end of the next section (see page 80). They can be used with either Black Letter alphabet.

Rounded Black Letter

Here is what the lower case Rounded Black Letter alphabet looks like:

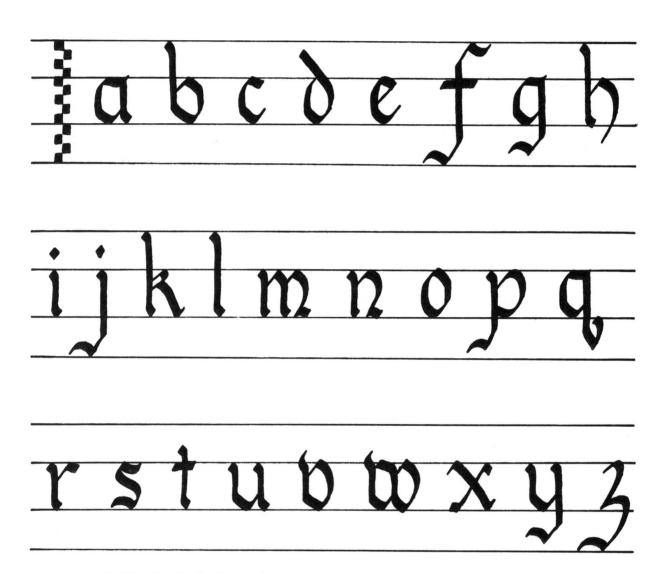

This alphabet is similar to Straight Black Letter in many ways. Many of the letters are still tall and basically straight, and the vertical lines are not slanted. But there are some important differences. The letters, though still more angular than Italics, are slightly more rounded than in Straight Black Letter. Some of the letters are formed differently, and the proportion is not quite the same. The main parts of the letters are 5 pen widths high, the ascenders are still 4 pen widths high, but the descenders now go 3 or 4 pen widths below the base line.

Use you own judgment when deciding how long to make your descenders. You can extend them as far as 5 pen widths if you wish, or keep them 3 pen widths long as you did in the Straight Black Letter alphabet. How angular or round you make your letters is also up to you. You will learn this alphabet in five lessons.

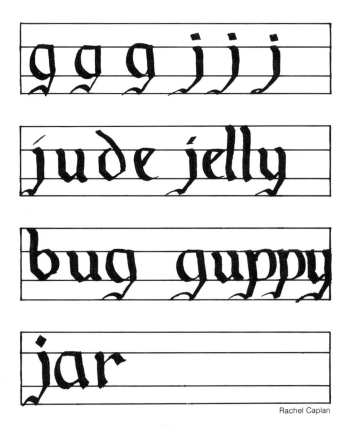

Rachel Caplan

Lesson 1: l,i,t,r,n,m,h.

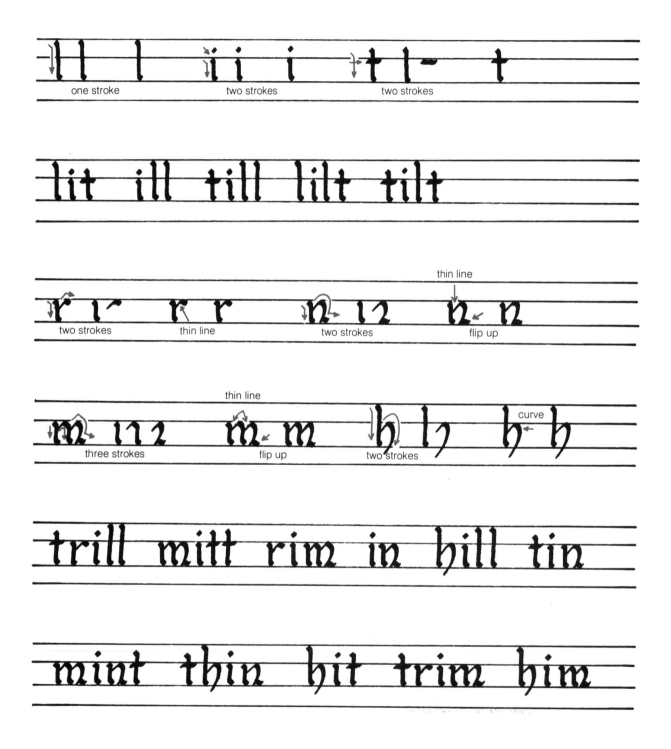

one stroke   two strokes   two strokes

lit ill till lilt tilt

thin line

two strokes   thin line   two strokes   flip up

thin line   curve

three strokes   flip up   two strokes

trill mitt rim in hill tin

mint thin hit trim him

Lesson 2: u, b, w.

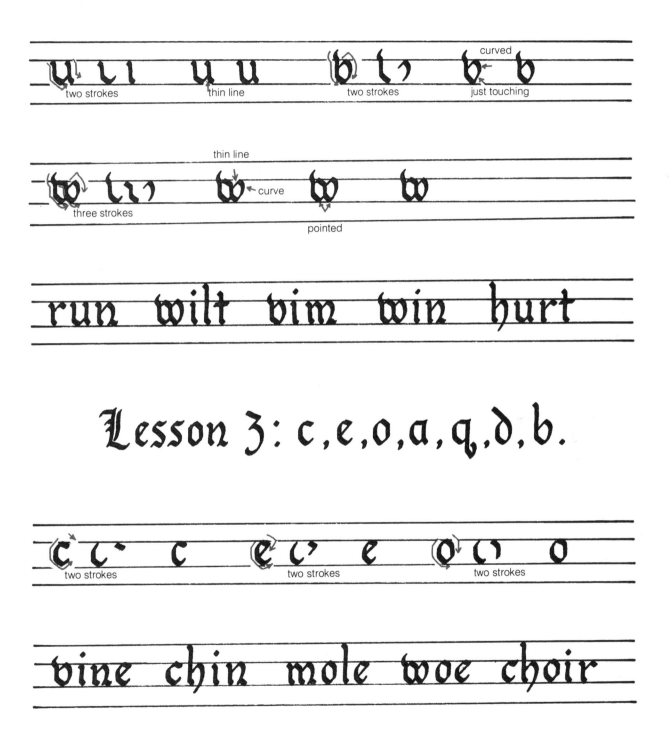

two strokes   thin line   two strokes   curved   just touching

thin line

three strokes   ← curve   pointed

run wilt bim win hurt

Lesson 3: c, e, o, a, q, d, b.

two strokes   two strokes   two strokes

vine chin mole woe choir

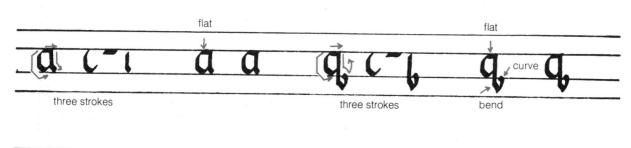

vane quote moat quell

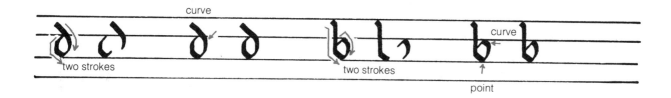

bad doe babble bawl red

Lesson 4: p, y, g, j, z, f.

You may make the descenders the same length if you wish.

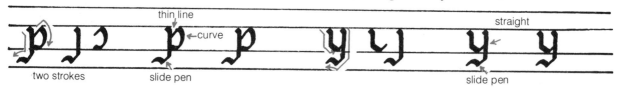

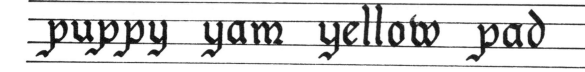

puppy yam yellow pad

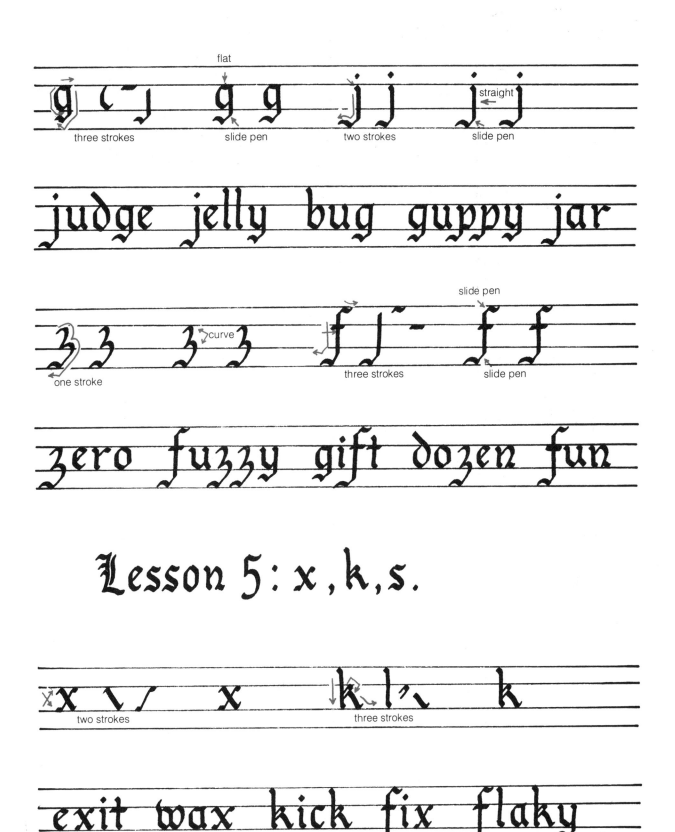

flat

three strokes   slide pen   two strokes   straight j   slide pen

judge jelly bug guppy jar

one stroke   curve   three strokes   slide pen   slide pen

zero fuzzy gift dozen fun

Lesson 5: x, k, s.

two strokes   three strokes

exit wax kick fix flaky

This is a difficult letter. Go slowly.

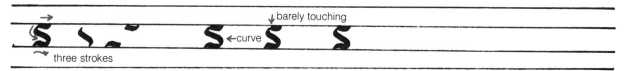

is mississippi first socks

a quick brown fox jumps

over the lazy dog

Before we learn the capitals, let us look at some alternatives to forming some of the lower case letters. Be consistent within each project in your use of whichever form you choose.

Alternate Forms of some letters
which can be used in either form of Black Letter:

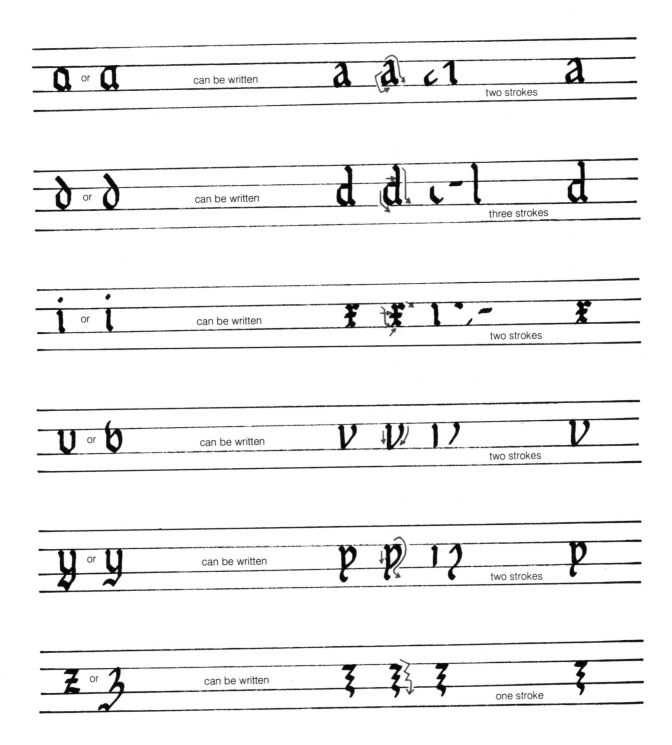

a or a   can be written   a a a cl   *two strokes*   a

d or d   can be written   d d cl   *three strokes*   d

i or i   can be written   *two strokes*

v or b   can be written   v v v   *two strokes*   v

y or y   can be written   p p p   *two strokes*   p

z or z   can be written   *one stroke*

Black Letter Capitals

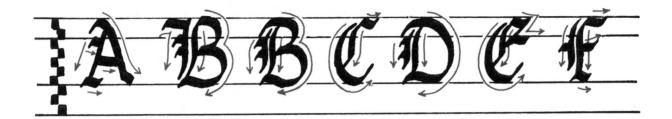

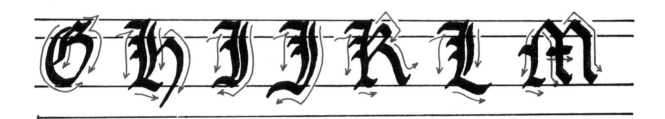

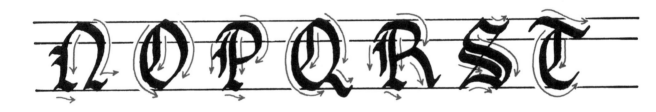

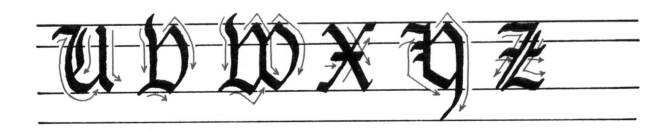

These capitals may be used with either style of Black Letter. Since they are so ornate, it is best not to write any words using only capitals. They go beautifully with Black Letter lower case letters. They are difficult to master, and they need to be practiced even more than the lower case letters, especially if you want them to look natural and flowing. You may also use them with the alphabets you have learned in the Italics section. They are about 7 pen widths high, as were the Italics capitals.

Practice them, change them, make them more elaborate or simplify them. Borrow ideas from other alphabets. It's up to you. These are suggestions based on traditional forms.

Alison Jordana Eve

Rachel Alyssa Tova

Hoté Mark Josh

Eve Rittenberg

Here are the capitals again, grouped by families:

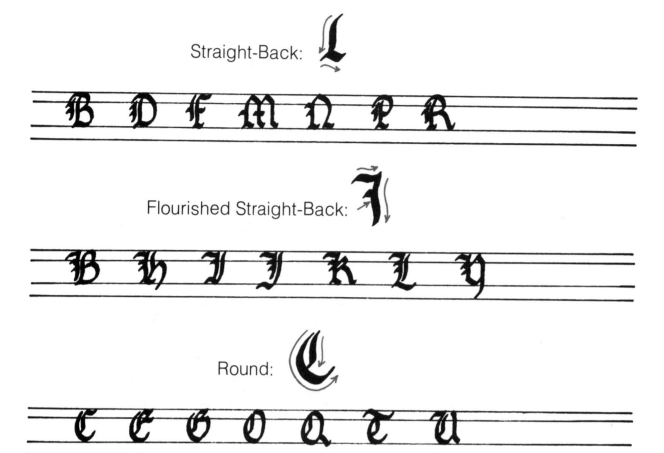

Straight-Back:

Flourished Straight-Back:

Round:

Special Letters:

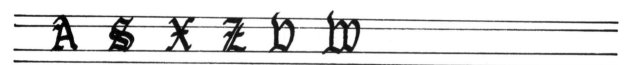

On the following page you will find some examples of other students' first attempts at Black Letter.

Samples of Black Letter

ccc cccc cc cccc

eeeeeeeeeeeee

o o o o o o o o o o o

bine chin mole quell

aaa aaaaaaaaaa

Liz Shilling

the quick brown fox
jumped over the
lazy dogs.

Eve Rittenberg

trill mitt

rim in hill

tin mint

hit trim

Betsy Schmidt

How to Use Calligraphy

The best way to practice calligraphy is to use it. At first you may want to use it only for very special projects. As you become more confident, however, you will use it more often. Write letters, make cards, write poetry. You will be happy with the results. Here are some examples of the uses of calligraphy:

Invitations:

You are cordially invited to a Birthday Party!

Place: 6 Oak Ave, Larchmont

Date: 5 o'clock till 7:30

Friday April 13th, 1979

Eve Rittenberg

Poetry:

Tomorrow

Tomorrow
I will meet
someone
　　special
who knows
　　what
it means to
　　be thirteen.

I will ask
this
　　special
　　　　Person
to
tell me if they
　　can please do
tell me if you
　　can please do
tell
　　me
how
　　to be
　　alive
　　　　and thirteen.

Perhaps
　　they will say
that I
must try to
　　stay
　　young
　　so that
I will
never
　　never
　　　　never
have to say
　　die.

Or that I
　　should
grow old and
　　　grey
and die away.

Or maybe
just
　　go fly
　　a kite

Lynn Stein

Signs:

Thank You
For Not
Smoking

Liz Shilling

cccccccccccccccccccccccccc

Clean enough to be
sanitary, yet dirty
enough to be liveable!

Janine's Room

Janine Amlung

85

Posters:

Come and See:
"My Fair Lady"
Date: May 17th   Performed by:
Time: 8:00pm.   the 3rd floor
Place: players
Chatsworth ave.
Auditorium

The American
Settlers of Texas,
having been under rule
of Mexican Govern-
ment, demand freedom of
Mexican rule. and recog-
nition of being a free Re-
public.

Quotations:

The fuzzy green elephant jumped
quickly on the brown varmint and
said "mmm, excellent!"

Greeting Cards:

Dear Ms. Baron,

Happy Birthday and best wishes. I hope you have a great year.

Love,
Hillary

Hillary Bogner

Placards:

Thou

shall close

thy cupboard

doors

Betsy Schmidt

Master for Italics

Do not write on this page. Use paper over it.

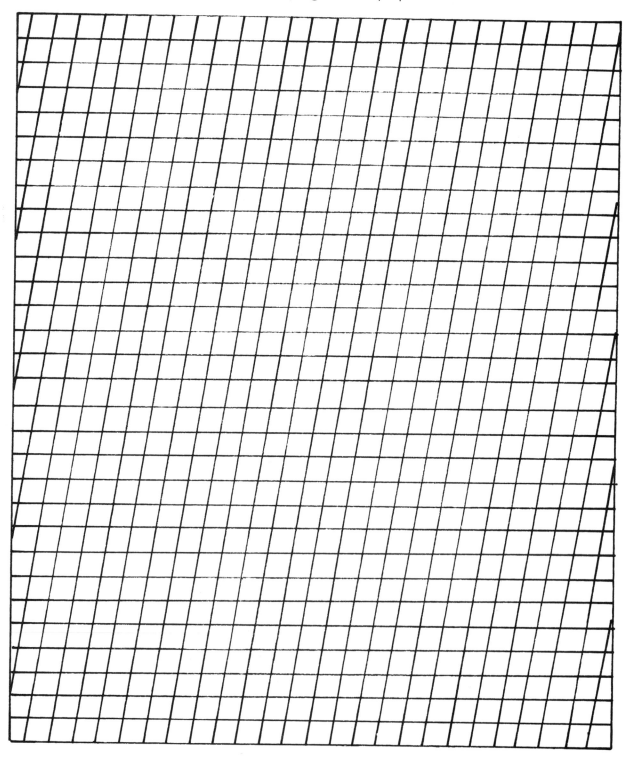

Master for Italics

Do not write on this page. Use paper over it.

Speedball C-2 or LC-2 nib

Master for Italics

Do not write on this page. Use paper over it.

Speedball C-4 or LC-4 nib
Platignum Broad nib

Master for Black Letter
Do not write on this page. Use paper over it.

Speedball C-2 or LC-2 nib

Master for Black Letter

Do not write on this page. Use paper over it.

Speedball C-4 or LC-4 nib
Platignum Broad nib

Appendix

Glossary

Ascender—the part of a letter that extends above the main body.

Calligraphy—the art of beautiful handwriting.

Descender—the part of a letter that extends below the main body.

Join—to connect letters, either by not lifting the pen, or by lifting the pen and then forming the new letters, making them touch at some point.

Letter body—the main part of the letter.

Letter families—grouping of letters that share similar characteristics.

Nib—part of the pen with the point.

Pen angle—angle made by the point of the pen and the guideline.

Point—the part of the pen that touches the paper.

List of Recommended Books

Ken Brown, *Calligraphy,* Volume I, Ken Brown Studio

Ralph Douglass, *Calligraphic Lettering with Pen and Brush,* Watson-Guptil Publications

Fred Eager, *The Italic Way to Beautiful Handwriting,* Mac-Millan Publishing Co.

Lloyd J. Reynolds, *Italic Calligraphy and Handwriting,* Pentalic Corporation

Margaret Shepherd, *Learning Calligraphy,* Wexford Press

Speedball Textbook of Pen and Brush Lettering, Hunt Manufacturing Co.

Charles Stoner, *Beautiful Italic Writing Made Easy,* Hunt Manufacturing Co.

Index